URSA

SPACE REVEALED

STARS & GALAXIES

by
Claudia Martin

Minneapolis, Minnesota

Credits

Cover and title page, © Space Telescope Science Institute Office of Public Outreach; Back Cover, © Skylines/Shutterstock; 5, © Science Photo Library/Alamy Stock; 6-7, © Andrea Danti/Shutterstock; 8TR, © Nerthuz/NASA/Shutterstock; 8MC, © Dotted Yeti/NASA/Shutterstock; 8MC, © Goddard Space Flight Center/Chris Smith (USRA)/NASA; 8MC, © Christina Krivonos/Shutterstock; 8BR, © Schlesinger Library, RIAS, Harvard University; 9, © Mohamed Elkhamisy/NASA/Shutterstock; 10-11, © BlueRingMedia/Shutterstock; 12MR, © Claus Lunau/Science Photo Library; 12BR, © isarescheewin/Shutterstock; 13, © grejak/NASA/Shutterstock; 14, © NASA/SDO/AIA/LMSAL; 15T, © NASA/SDO/Science Photo Library; 15M, © GSFC/SDO/NASA; 15B, © NASA/SDO/Science Photo Library; 16MR, © Mark Garlick/Science Photo Library; 16BR, © ESO/; 17, © ESA and the Hubble Heritage Team (STScI/AURA)/NASA; 18MR, © Wellcome Collection/; 18BR, © JPL-Caltech/NASA; 19, © PlanilAstro/Shutterstock; 20M, © Mark Garlick/Science Photo Library; 20BR, © Mark Garlick/Science Photo Library; 21T, © ESA, H. Bond (STScI)/NASA; 21M, © Julian Baum/Science Photo Library; 21B, © elladoro/Shutterstock; 22M, © Marusya Chaika/Shutterstock; 22BR, © Hollygraphic/Shutterstock; 23, © Bruce Rolff/Shutterstock; 24, © Elena11/NASA/Shutterstock; 25T, © C. Carreau/ESA; 25B, © Event Horizon Telescope collaboration et al./; 26M, © QA International/Science Source/Science Photo Library; 26BR, © WENN/Alamy Stock; 27, © NASA images/Shutterstock; 28MR, © NASA images/Shutterstock; 28BL, © Allexxandar/NASA/Shutterstock; 29TR, © Dr Rudolph Schild/Science Photo Library; 29ML, © ESA and the Hubble Heritage Team (STScI/AURA)/NASA; 29BL, © The Hubble Heritage Team (STScI/AURA/NASA; 30-31, © Mark Garlick/Science Photo Library/Alamy Stock; 31TR, © Kevin Key/Shutterstock; 32MR, © Library of Congress/Science Photo Library; 32BR, © Catmando/Shutterstock; 33, © NASA images/Shutterstock; 34, © Dotted Yeti/Shutterstock; 35TL, © AleksandrMorrisovich/Shutterstock; 35TR, © Dotted Yeti/Shutterstock; 35MR, © NASA images/Shutterstock; 35B, © JPL-Caltech/NASA; 36MR, © Sidney Hall/Library of Congress; 36BR, © W4sm astro/Shutterstock; 37, © NASA images/Shutterstock; 38MR, © Mikkel Juul Jensen/Science Photo Library; 38BR, © Hubble/NASA; 39, © NASA images/Shutterstock; 40MR, © Mark Garlick/Science Photo Library; 40BR, © Hubble Space Telescope & NASA/ESA; 41, © Mark Garlick/Science Photo Library; 42-43, © 24K-Production/Adobe Stock; 44MR, © Science Photo Library/Alamy Stock; 45TR, © NASA images/Shutterstock; 45B, © Mark Garlick/Science Photo Library/Alamy Stock; 47B, © Mark Garlick/Science Photo Library

Bearport Publishing Company Product Development Team

President: Jen Jenson; Director of Product Development: Spencer Brinker; Managing Editor: Allison Juda; Associate Editor: Naomi Reich; Associate Editor: Tiana Tran; Art Director: Colin O'Dea; Designer: Kim Jones; Designer: Kayla Eggert; Product Development Assistant: Owen Hamlin

Statement on Usage of Generative Artificial Intelligence

Bearport Publishing remains committed to publishing high-quality nonfiction books. Therefore, we restrict the use of generative AI to ensure accuracy of all text and visual components pertaining to a book's subject. See BearportPublishing.com for details.

Library of Congress Cataloging-in-Publication Data is available at www.loc.gov or upon request from the publisher.

ISBN: 979-8-89232-081-8 (hardcover)
ISBN: 979-8-89232-613-1 (paperback)
ISBN: 979-8-89232-214-0 (ebook)

© 2025 Arcturus Holdings Limited
This edition is published by arrangement with Arcturus Publishing Limited.

North American adaptations © 2025 Bearport Publishing Company. All rights reserved. No part of this publication may be reproduced in whole or in part, stored in any retrieval system, or transmitted in any form or by any means, electronic, mechanical, photocopying, recording, or otherwise, without written permission from the publisher. Bearport Publishing is a division of Chrysalis Education Group.

For more information, write to Bearport Publishing, 5357 Penn Avenue South, Minneapolis, MN 55419.

CONTENTS

Stuff of the Universe.................... 4
The Big Bang........................... 6
Stars.................................. 8
Star Types............................ 10
The Sun 12
Solar Activity......................... 14
The Pillars of Creation................. 16
The Seven Sisters..................... 18
Star Systems 20
The Clown Face Nebula 22
Black Holes........................... 24
Universe of Galaxies 26
Galaxy Types 28
The Milky Way........................ 30
The Andromeda Galaxy 32
Exoplanets 34
The Antennae Galaxies................ 36
Centaurus A.......................... 38
The Laniakea Supercluster 40
An Expanding Future 42

Review and Reflect 44
Glossary.............................. 46
Read More............................ 47
Learn More Online.................... 47
Index 48

STUFF OF THE UNIVERSE

The universe burst into being as a single point of extremely dense, compact, and superheated atomic particles that suddenly exploded—an event known as the Big Bang. Immediately after, the universe began to stretch and inflate. For just a fraction of a second, the universe was spreading faster than the speed of light before beginning to slow and cool. Matter and radiation, or heat energy, began to fill the expanding space. Over time, these formed everything that now fills the universe—atoms, planets, moons, stars, and galaxies.

The universe continues to grow and stretch through the present day, and some scientists think it will expand forever. It is almost impossible to conceive of the universe's enormous size. Earth is only one of 40 billion planets in our galaxy—a huge collection of dust, gas, and billions of stars. The sun is just one medium-sized star among 200 trillion billion stars in the universe. Our solar system is one of more than 3,200 in the Milky Way Galaxy, which is only one of as many as 2 trillion galaxies in the universe.

Everything we can observe and measure in a galaxy is the product of the universe's initial burst of heat, pressure, and movement. By studying galaxies and all they contain, we can learn a little more about the creation of our universe. We can gaze back in time to see how they came to be. We can also look forward to predict what they will become and, perhaps, how they will come to an end.

Taken together, galaxies and the stars they contain are the stuff of the universe. They are changing records of the universe's past, present, and future. By studying stars and galaxies, we can begin to grasp the enormity of all that surrounds us.

THE BIG BANG

Astronomers believe the universe was born 13.8 billion years ago in an event called the Big Bang. In its first moment, the universe began to expand from a single point—and has been expanding ever since. The Big Bang brought space and time into existence, but no one knows why it happened or what, if anything, existed before.

TIMELINE: FROM THE BIG BANG TO TODAY

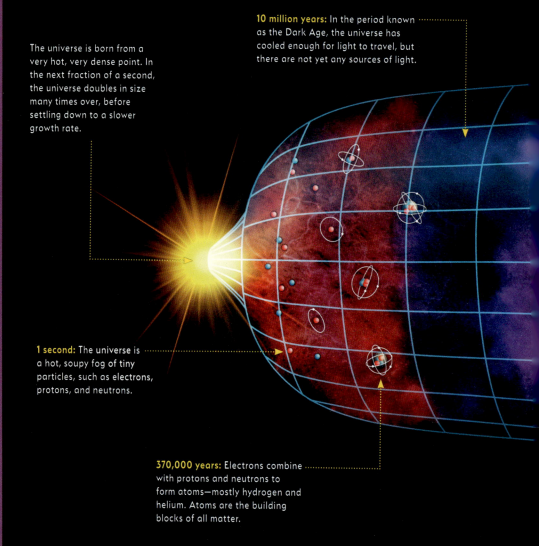

The universe is born from a very hot, very dense point. In the next fraction of a second, the universe doubles in size many times over, before settling down to a slower growth rate.

10 million years: In the period known as the Dark Age, the universe has cooled enough for light to travel, but there are not yet any sources of light.

1 second: The universe is a hot, soupy fog of tiny particles, such as electrons, protons, and neutrons.

370,000 years: Electrons combine with protons and neutrons to form atoms—mostly hydrogen and helium. Atoms are the building blocks of all matter.

Most astronomers think the Big Bang theory is correct because when they scan the sky, they can detect the remains of heat from the Big Bang in the form of energy called microwaves. They also study how the universe is growing and then use math to project backward to the moment when it was a single point.

Astronomers have many different theories about what will happen to the universe in the future. Most believe it will continue to expand forever. However, some think the universe will end in a Big Crunch, when it will shrink back to a single point. A Big Bounce might follow, with the expansion starting all over again.

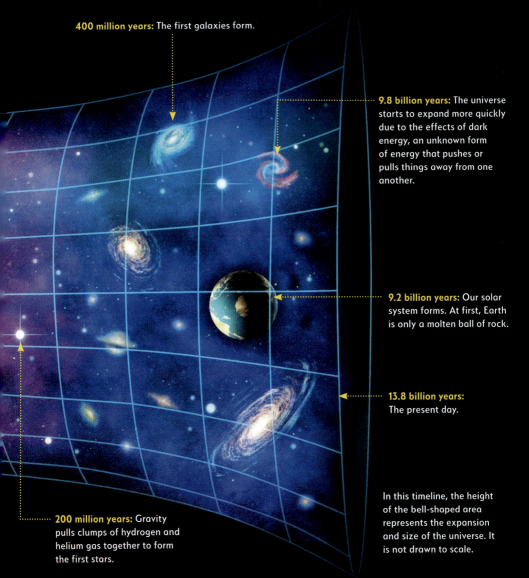

400 million years: The first galaxies form.

9.8 billion years: The universe starts to expand more quickly due to the effects of dark energy, an unknown form of energy that pushes or pulls things away from one another.

9.2 billion years: Our solar system forms. At first, Earth is only a molten ball of rock.

13.8 billion years: The present day.

200 million years: Gravity pulls clumps of hydrogen and helium gas together to form the first stars.

In this timeline, the height of the bell-shaped area represents the expansion and size of the universe. It is not drawn to scale.

STARS

Most of the glowing dots we see in the night sky are stars. Apart from the sun, our nearest star, they are all trillions of miles away. Astronomers think there may be one septillion (1 followed by 24 zeros) stars in the universe. Most of them are too distant to be seen by the naked eye.

Stars are glowing balls of gas, mostly hydrogen and helium. The gas has become so hot that it transformed into plasma, a gas-like state of matter. Like everything else, plasma is made of tiny atoms. In plasma, these atoms are so hot that particles called electrons break away. Each electron carries a tiny electric charge, which gives plasma an electric charge.

A star is hot and glowing because its hydrogen atoms are constantly crashing together in its core. These collisions create helium atoms and release energy in the form of light and heat. All stars eventually run out of hydrogen. Without this fuel, they begin to change and eventually die.

A star is held together by its own gravity, the force that pulls all objects toward one another. A star's gravity may also hold other objects in orbit around it. Our sun keeps all the objects in the solar system spinning around it. The sun is far from the only star with orbiting planets. Astronomers estimate there are billions of other solar systems in the universe.

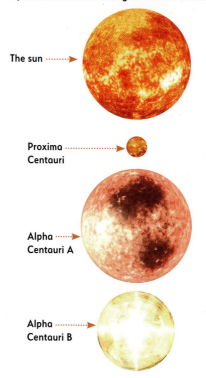

The three closest stars to the sun are Proxima Centauri, Alpha Centauri A, and Alpha Centauri B. Alpha Centauri A is the largest of the four stars.

The sun

Proxima Centauri

Alpha Centauri A

Alpha Centauri B

Star Spectrum

The light that human eyes can see is made up of all colors of the rainbow, known as the visible spectrum. If a star is very hot, its light is bluer. If it is cooler, its light looks more red. The astronomer Annie Jump Cannon helped develop the system of classifying stars by their temperature and color.

Annie Jump Cannon (1863–1941) put stars into classes O, B, A, F, G, K, and M, with O being the hottest.

The light from star V838 Monocerotis (shown in red) is reflecting off clouds of gas and dust in this photograph taken by the Hubble Space Telescope.

STAR TYPES

The heavier a star, the hotter and brighter it is. The lightest stars are red and relatively dim. Medium stars are yellow, while the heaviest are often blue and very bright. Smaller stars are usually called dwarfs, while large stars are known as giants or supergiants.

For most of its life, a star is in a period known as the main sequence. This is the time when it is turning hydrogen into helium in its core, and there is a balance between gravity trying to shrink it and heat making it grow. A star will remain in this stable stage of its life until it runs out of hydrogen. Most main sequence stars are dwarf stars.

The heavier the star, the faster it uses up its store of hydrogen. The largest stars may last for only a few million years, while the smallest might survive for 10 trillion years! This is many times longer than the 13.8 billion years the universe has existed. When a larger main sequence star runs out of hydrogen, it swells into a red giant or a supergiant. A smaller main sequence star shrinks into a white dwarf, around one-hundredth the size of the sun.

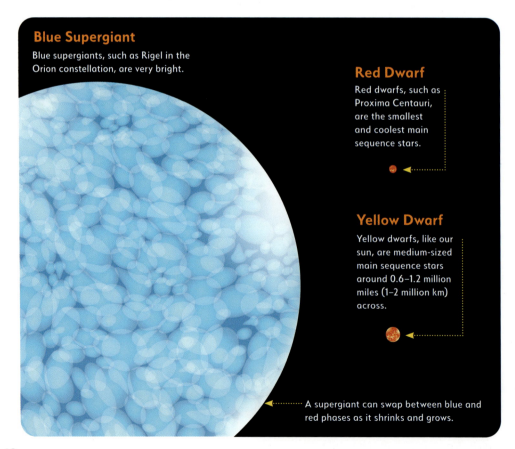

Blue Supergiant
Blue supergiants, such as Rigel in the Orion constellation, are very bright.

Red Dwarf
Red dwarfs, such as Proxima Centauri, are the smallest and coolest main sequence stars.

Yellow Dwarf
Yellow dwarfs, like our sun, are medium-sized main sequence stars around 0.6–1.2 million miles (1–2 million km) across.

A supergiant can swap between blue and red phases as it shrinks and grows.

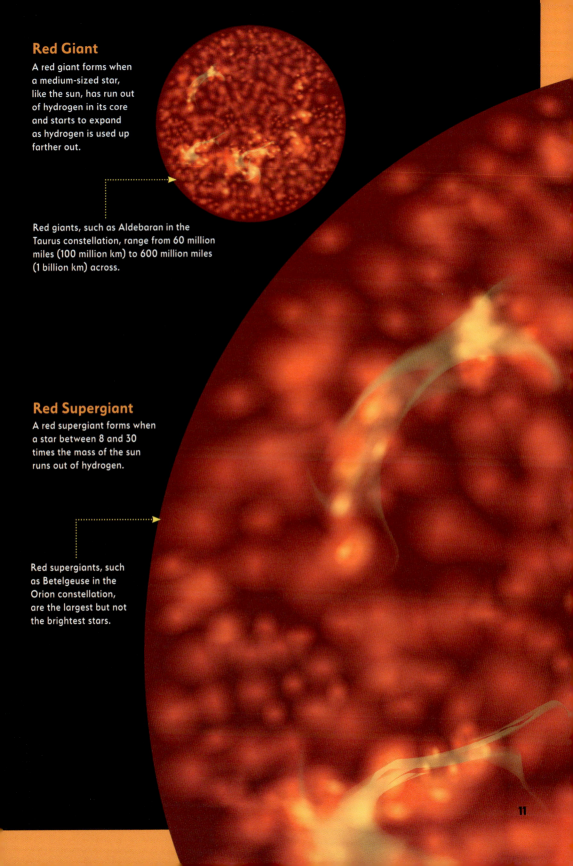

Red Giant

A red giant forms when a medium-sized star, like the sun, has run out of hydrogen in its core and starts to expand as hydrogen is used up farther out.

Red giants, such as Aldebaran in the Taurus constellation, range from 60 million miles (100 million km) to 600 million miles (1 billion km) across.

Red Supergiant

A red supergiant forms when a star between 8 and 30 times the mass of the sun runs out of hydrogen.

Red supergiants, such as Betelgeuse in the Orion constellation, are the largest but not the brightest stars.

THE SUN

The sun is a medium-sized yellow dwarf star, although its light is white rather than yellow. The star formed around 4.57 billion years ago and is likely to survive another 5 billion years. The sun's heat and light enable life to flourish on Earth. Without the sun, plants could not grow and animals would not find food.

In the sun's core, hydrogen atoms are constantly fusing into helium. This releases energy, which travels outward to the sun's surface. First, it travels through the radiative zone. It moves by a process called radiation, where the energy is carried by tiny particles named photons. After about 170,000 years, the energy reaches the convection zone. Here, bubbles of hot plasma carry the energy by convection. This means they rise to the surface like boiling water in a pan.

The surface of the sun is called the photosphere. It gives off energy in the form of sunlight and heat, which reaches Earth about eight minutes later. Above the photosphere is the sun's atmosphere, which astronomers divide into the chromosphere and the outer corona.

When the sun runs out of hydrogen in its core in around five billion years, its outer layers will expand, transforming the star into a red giant. This process will swallow Mercury and Venus—and fry Earth. The sun will spend half a billion years as a red giant, while it uses its helium atoms as fuel. Eventually, when the helium is gone, the sun will shed its outer layers and become a white dwarf. It will slowly cool down over billions or trillions of years.

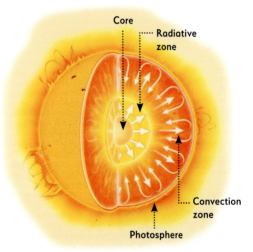

The sun's core reaches around 27 million degrees Fahrenheit (15 million degrees Celsius).

The Sun

Type: Yellow dwarf star
Size: 0.86 million miles (1.39 million km) across
Mass: The same as 333,000 Earths
Age: 4.57 billion years
Surface temperature: 10,000°F (5,500°C)
Distance from Milky Way core: 27,200 light-years

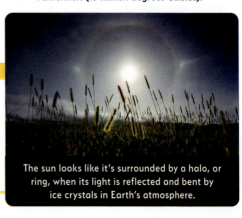

The sun looks like it's surrounded by a halo, or ring, when its light is reflected and bent by ice crystals in Earth's atmosphere.

The sun's light is so bright it can blind human eyes, but the cameras of the Solar Dynamics Observatory take photos that let us see its features in detail.

SOLAR ACTIVITY

With dark sunspots and sudden explosions of energy called flares, the sun's surface is extremely active. This solar activity is caused by magnetism, a force created by the movement of electric charges. The amount of solar activity changes through an 11-year period known as the solar cycle.

Every substance is made of atoms. Each atom has particles called electrons circling its nucleus, or core. Electrons carry electric charges. Their movement creates an electric current and makes each electron behave like a tiny magnet. In a star's plasma, the electrons have been completely separated from their atoms, creating areas of powerful magnetic forces called magnetic fields. Since the plasma is constantly moving, the magnetic fields twist and tangle. This creates the activity on the sun's surface.

The sun has a north and a south magnetic pole. These are the locations on a star or planet where the magnetic field lines are vertical, pointing either downward (the north pole) or upward (the south pole). Every 11 years, the sun's north and south poles swap places. This swap happens when solar activity is busiest. At these times, intense flares and bursts of charged particles fly off into space. This solar activity is so powerful it can damage Earth's radio communications and electricity supplies.

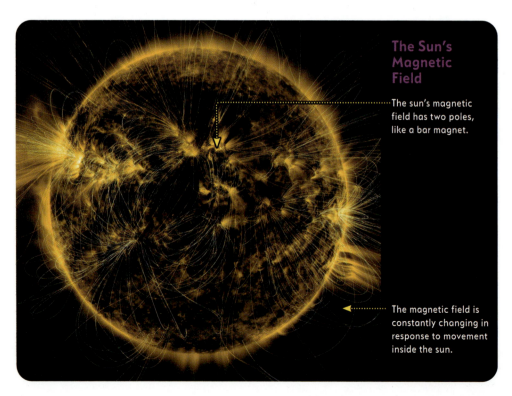

The Sun's Magnetic Field

The sun's magnetic field has two poles, like a bar magnet.

The magnetic field is constantly changing in response to movement inside the sun.

14

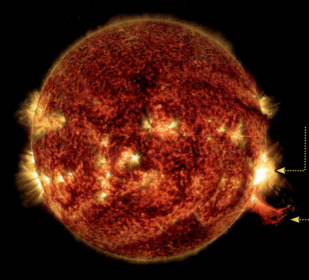

Solar Flare
A solar flare is a burst of light, heat, and other energy caused by the tangling of magnetic field lines.

Material from the sun erupts into space.

Sunspots
This image from the Solar Dynamics Observatory is created from photographs and information about magnetic activity.

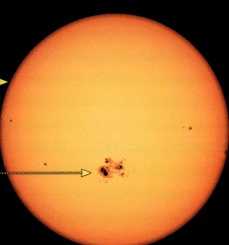

Sunspots, which appear and disappear, are cooler areas caused by magnetic field lines stopping hot plasma from rising to the surface.

Coronal Loop
A coronal loop can be seen when a loop of magnetic field traps glowing plasma.

THE PILLARS OF CREATION

About 5,700 light-years from Earth is a cloud of dust and gas called the Eagle Nebula. This nebula is home to several stellar nurseries, including the Pillars of Creation. These thick areas of cloud are where new stars are born. Scientists believe the process of star formation takes more than 10 million years. Across the universe, about 400 million stars are born every day.

A new star forms in a thick cloud of dust mixed with hydrogen and helium gas. A clump starts to grow in the cloud, caused by a collision with another cloud or the solar wind from a nearby star. As the clump grows, its gravity pulls more dust and gas into a ball. Eventually, the ball gets so big that it collapses in on itself. This collapse makes the material in the center of the ball heat up. When it reaches 27 million°F (15 million°C), 4 hydrogen atoms start to join together to form helium atoms. This releases an immense amount of energy and a new, shining star is born.

The Pillars of Creation are thick clouds shaped like large columns. These kinds of tall pillars often form at the edges of nebulae. The tallest pillar is 5 light-years long, much larger than our entire solar system. Hidden inside the pillars are newborn and newly forming stars. The energy from all its bright young stars makes the gases in the Eagle Nebula glow. A nebula that gives off light in this way is known as an emission nebula.

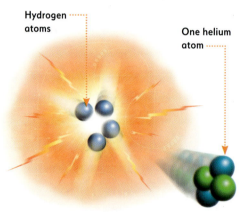

A process called nuclear fusion takes place in a star's core. This is when four hydrogen atoms come together to form one helium atom.

The Eagle Nebula

Type: Emission nebula
Size: 70 light-years across
Mass: The same as 12,000 suns
Age: 1–2 million years
Average temperature: -450°F (-270°C)
Distance from the sun: 5,700 light-years

Energy from newborn stars makes the Eagle Nebula's hydrogen gas glow red. The Pillars of Creation are near the middle of the photograph.

The darker areas in the Pillars of Creation are clumps where new stars are forming.

17

THE SEVEN SISTERS

The Seven Sisters, also known as the Pleiades, is an open star cluster, or group of stars that formed from the same cloud and are about the same age. These stars are loosely held together by the pull of their gravity. The cluster contains around 1,000 stars, but only 14 can be seen by the naked eye from Earth.

The stars in the Seven Sisters probably formed around 115 million years ago. The stars that can be easily seen from Earth are bright, very hot, and blue. Most of the cluster's other stars are fainter and red. The cluster also contains many brown dwarfs, starlike objects that are too small for hydrogen atoms to fuse in their core.

The Seven Sisters cluster will stay together for around another 250 million years, but then they will be pulled apart by the gravity of other stars or nebulae. In contrast, globular star clusters stay together for billions of years. Globular clusters contain many more stars, are more sphere-like in shape, and are much more tightly bound by gravity than open clusters.

The Seven Sisters gets its name from Greek mythology. The cluster's nine brightest stars are named after seven mythological sisters as well as their parents, Atlas and Pleione. According to the myths, the god Atlas was forced to carry the sky on his shoulders. To comfort him, the king of the gods, Zeus, turned his daughters into stars to keep him company.

The Seven Sisters can be seen in the constellation of Taurus, the bull, shown here in a 19th-century star chart.

The Seven Sisters

Type: Open star cluster
Size: 16 light-years across
Mass: The same as 800 suns
Age: 115 million years
Surface temperature of brightest star: 21,600°F (12,000°C)
Distance from the sun: 445 light-years

In this infrared image of the Seven Sisters, the thickest clouds of dust are shown in yellow and red, while thinner dust is green.

The brightest star in the Seven Sisters is Alcyone, which is 10 times the size of the sun.

STAR SYSTEMS

A star system is a small group of stars that orbit one another. A star system is much smaller than a star cluster or a galaxy, which can contain hundreds to trillions of stars. Most star systems are binary systems, containing two stars, or triple systems, containing three. However, groups of up to nine stars have been found.

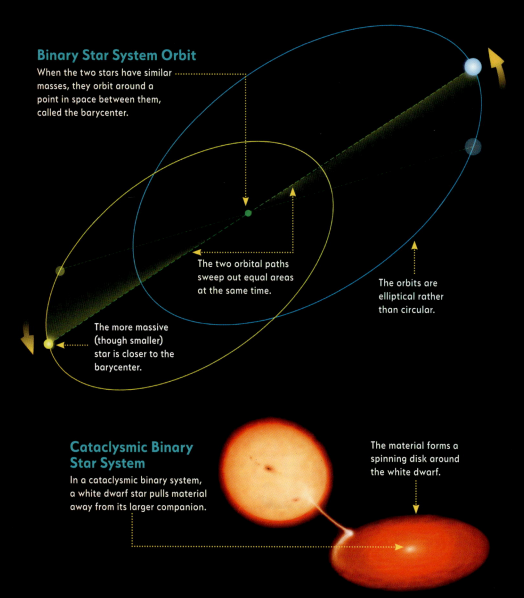

Binary Star System Orbit

When the two stars have similar masses, they orbit around a point in space between them, called the barycenter.

The two orbital paths sweep out equal areas at the same time.

The orbits are elliptical rather than circular.

The more massive (though smaller) star is closer to the barycenter.

Cataclysmic Binary Star System

In a cataclysmic binary system, a white dwarf star pulls material away from its larger companion.

The material forms a spinning disk around the white dwarf.

Sirius A and Sirius B Binary Star System

This Hubble Space Telescope photograph shows the binary system of Sirius A and Sirius B, which orbit each other every 50 years.

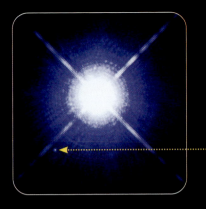

Sirius B is a small white dwarf, lying around 1.9 billion miles (3 billion km) from its larger partner.

Alpha Centauri Triple Star System

In this illustration, our sun is surrounded by the Oort Cloud ring of objects.

Proxima Centauri, the nearest star to the sun, makes one orbit of Alpha Centauri A and B every 555,000 years.

Alpha Centauri A and Alpha Centauri B orbit each other once every 80 years.

Sirius A

Type: Blue-white dwarf star
Size: 1.48 million miles (2.38 million km) across
Mass: The same as 2 suns
Age: 250 million years
Surface temperature: 17,500°F (9,700°C)
Distance from the sun: 8.6 light-years

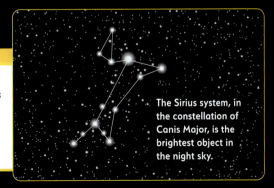

The Sirius system, in the constellation of Canis Major, is the brightest object in the night sky.

THE CLOWN FACE NEBULA

The Clown Face Nebula is a glowing cloud of gas and dust. It is a planetary nebula, but it was not formed by a planet. The cloud was thrown out by a dying red giant star. The Clown Face Nebula is one of about 3,000 planetary nebulae in our Milky Way Galaxy.

All planetary nebulae are formed by red giant stars. Only medium-sized stars, between around 0.3 and 8 times the mass of our sun, become red giants when they run out of hydrogen fuel. Smaller stars shrink straight into white dwarfs, while larger stars explode as supernovae. Toward the end of its life, our sun will form a planetary nebula.

When a sunlike star runs out of hydrogen, its outer layers expand, turning it into a red giant. At the same time, the star's core shrinks and heats up, until it is hot enough for helium atoms to fuse into carbon and oxygen atoms. This releases huge amounts of energy, pushing the star's atmosphere out into space.

The gases from the atmosphere form a cloud around the dying star, whose light makes the gases glow. This planetary nebula will last for only around 10,000 years before the gases drift away. At the same time, the star runs out of helium. Without its fuel, the remains of the star, known as a white dwarf, slowly cool and fade over trillions of years.

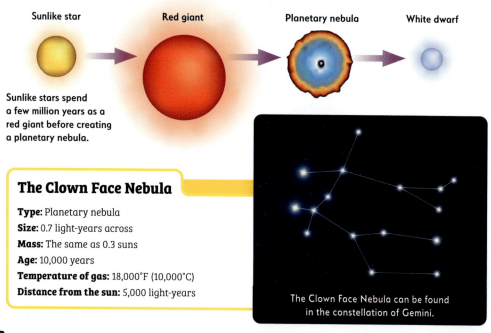

Sunlike star → Red giant → Planetary nebula → White dwarf

Sunlike stars spend a few million years as a red giant before creating a planetary nebula.

The Clown Face Nebula

Type: Planetary nebula
Size: 0.7 light-years across
Mass: The same as 0.3 suns
Age: 10,000 years
Temperature of gas: 18,000°F (10,000°C)
Distance from the sun: 5,000 light-years

The Clown Face Nebula can be found in the constellation of Gemini.

A white dwarf star can be seen at the heart of the nebula. The surrounding bubble and feathery streaks are formed by gases as they are blown away.

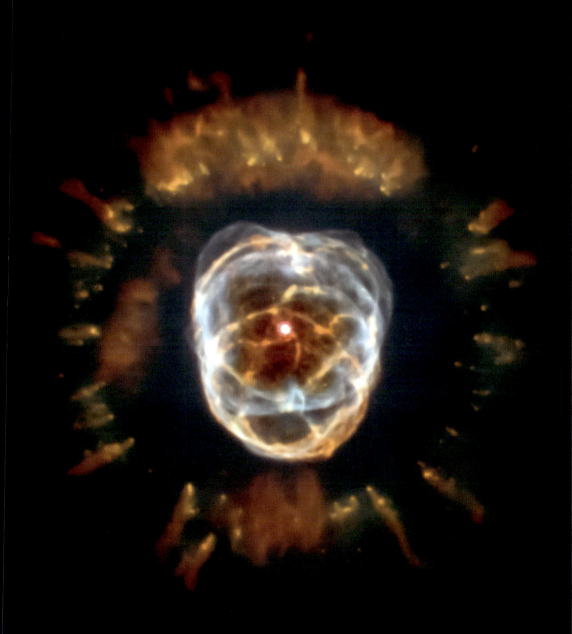

BLACK HOLES

A black hole is a region of space where gravity is so strong that almost nothing can escape its pull. If a star, a planet, or even light crosses the boundary known as a black hole's event horizon, it will be sucked inside. Black holes can form when an extremely massive star collapses in a supernova.

The larger an object's mass, the greater the pull of its gravity. If enough mass is squeezed into a small enough space, its gravity can warp space—creating a black hole. This can happen when a star more than 20 times the mass of the sun runs out of fuel and collapses in on itself. Such black holes, known as stellar black holes, have a mass from 5 to 100 times that of our sun. Once a black hole has formed, it can grow by sucking in surrounding gas, dust, planets, and stars.

A supermassive black hole has a mass millions or billions of times larger than the sun's. Scientists believe a supermassive black hole lies at the core of most galaxies. Supermassive black holes may have formed from growing stellar black holes, from many black holes merging, from the collapse of whole star clusters, or from the collapse of gas clouds early in the life of the universe.

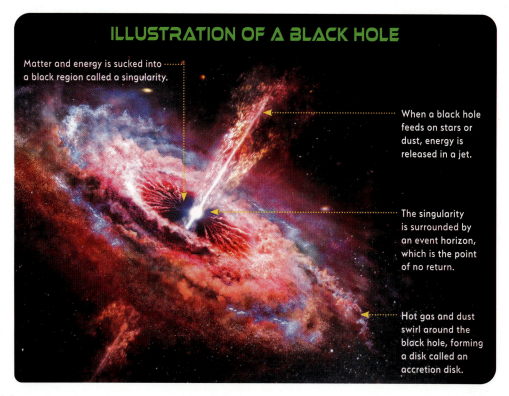

ILLUSTRATION OF A BLACK HOLE

Matter and energy is sucked into a black region called a singularity.

When a black hole feeds on stars or dust, energy is released in a jet.

The singularity is surrounded by an event horizon, which is the point of no return.

Hot gas and dust swirl around the black hole, forming a disk called an accretion disk.

24

Sagittarius A* Supermassive Black Hole

At the core of our Milky Way Galaxy is a supermassive black hole with a mass four million times that of our sun.

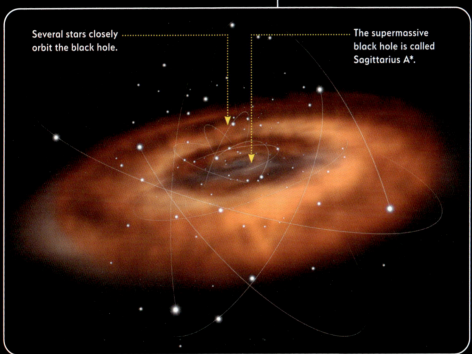

Several stars closely orbit the black hole.

The supermassive black hole is called Sagittarius A*.

First Photo of a Black Hole

The Event Horizon Telescope captured this image of the supermassive black hole at the core of galaxy M87.

We can see the black hole **only** because of the hot gas swirling around its event horizon.

25

UNIVERSE OF GALAXIES

A galaxy is a collection of stars, planets, gas, and dust that is held together by gravity. The Milky Way is our own galaxy, and it is one of as many as two trillion galaxies in the universe. Galaxies usually group together into clusters and larger superclusters.

Everything with mass has gravity. Gravity from the mass of the stars and other matter in a galaxy keeps it together. Everything in a galaxy spins around a central point, in the same way the planets in our solar system spin around the sun. Astronomers believe that at the center of most galaxies there is a supermassive black hole with extremely powerful gravity.

Most galaxies are 3,000 to 300,000 light-years across. The stars nearest our sun are usually no closer than 4 light-years apart, but in the core of a galaxy they can be 300 times closer. Most galaxies are separated from one another by at least three million light-years. The space between galaxies is not entirely empty, however. There is less than one atom of gas in each cubic yard (0.8 cubic m) of space. This is called the intergalactic medium.

Astronomers are not sure how the first galaxies formed. It is possible that immense clumps of gas and dust collapsed, forming all the stars of a galaxy nearly at once. Another theory is that clusters of stars formed first, then grouped together afterward.

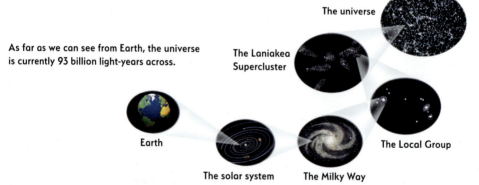

As far as we can see from Earth, the universe is currently 93 billion light-years across.

Earth — The solar system — The Milky Way — The Local Group — The Laniakea Supercluster — The universe

Dark Matter

Matter is any substance, from an atom to a planet, that occupies space and has mass. However, around 85 percent of the matter in the universe is invisible. We know this dark matter exists because of the effects of its gravity. Astronomer Vera Rubin calculated that there must be a lot of dark matter within galaxies, because without its gravity, galaxies would fly apart.

Vera Rubin (1928–2016) found the first proof of dark matter.

Around 23 million light-years from Earth, the spiral Whirlpool Galaxy has a smaller companion galaxy (*top*) named NGC 5195.

GALAXY TYPES

Galaxies range in size from dwarfs with a few hundred million stars to giants with a hundred trillion stars. Most galaxies are dwarfs and often orbit around a larger galaxy. Astronomers group galaxies into three main shapes: spiral, elliptical, and irregular.

Spiral galaxies have huge flat arms of bright young stars that turn around a central bulge of older stars. Some spiral galaxies, called barred spirals, have a bar-shaped band of stars that stretches to either side of the core, then blends into the spiral arms.

Elliptical galaxies are roughly the shape of a ball that has been flattened a little. They usually contain old stars. Elliptical galaxies can be any size, but the largest galaxies in the universe are all elliptical. They may have been formed when two or more galaxies collided and merged.

Around a quarter of galaxies do not have an elliptical or spiral shape. Irregular galaxies are usually dwarfs. They may have been pulled out of shape by the gravity of a larger galaxy nearby. Some galaxies, such as ring galaxies, have a peculiar shape because of a collision.

Spiral
The Pinwheel Galaxy has about 1 trillion stars and is 170,000 light-years across.

Barred Spiral
The barred spiral galaxy known as NGC 1300 lies about 61 million light-years from Earth.

Elliptical
This image of galaxy M105 shows its hottest areas in yellow and its coolest in green.

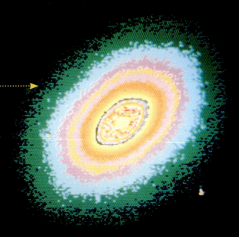

Irregular
NGC 1427A is a dwarf irregular galaxy that is being pulled by the gravity of several nearby galaxies and will one day break apart.

Ring
Hoag's Object is a ring galaxy that was formed two to three billion years ago when a small galaxy plunged through the heart of a larger disk-shaped galaxy.

29

THE MILKY WAY

Our solar system is in a barred spiral galaxy known as the Milky Way. The stars, gas, and dust of the galaxy rotate around its core at different speeds, with the arms taking between 220 and 360 million years to make one orbit. Several smaller galaxies, called satellite galaxies, are in orbit around the Milky Way. The largest is the Large Magellanic Cloud, which can be found about 163,000 light-years away.

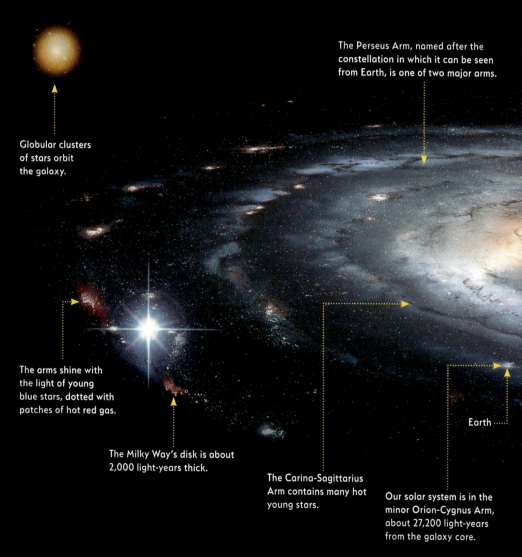

The Perseus Arm, named after the constellation in which it can be seen from Earth, is one of two major arms.

Globular clusters of stars orbit the galaxy.

The arms shine with the light of young blue stars, dotted with patches of hot red gas.

The Milky Way's disk is about 2,000 light-years thick.

The Carina-Sagittarius Arm contains many hot young stars.

Earth

Our solar system is in the minor Orion-Cygnus Arm, about 27,200 light-years from the galaxy core.

The Milky Way

Type: Barred spiral galaxy
Size: 170,000–200,000 light-years across
Number of stars: 100–400 billion
Mass of supermassive black hole: The same as 10 million suns
Satellite galaxies: More than 50
Average rotation speed: 130 miles per second (210 kps)

Our galaxy can be seen as a pale milky band of light in the night sky, which is how it got its name.

The exact shape of the galaxy's arms is difficult to know because, from Earth, we cannot see across the tightly packed, dusty core to the other side.

The central bar is home to some of the oldest and yellowest stars, up to 13.5 billion years old, as well as a supermassive black hole called Sagittarius A*.

The major Scutum-Centaurus Arm spirals outward from the end of the central bar nearest Earth.

THE ANDROMEDA GALAXY

The Andromeda Galaxy is a barred spiral that formed 10 billion years ago when smaller galaxies collided. Today, Andromeda and the Milky Way are the two largest galaxies in a group known as the Local Group. There are at least 80 other galaxies in the group, all held near one another by gravity.

On a moonless night, the Andromeda Galaxy is bright enough to be seen with the naked eye in the constellation of Andromeda. The constellation was named after a princess in Greek mythology who was chained to a rock to be eaten by a sea monster. Andromeda was rescued by the hero Perseus, who appears in a nearby constellation.

In 964 CE, Persian astronomer Abd al-Rahman al-Sufi was the first to record findings about the Andromeda Galaxy, which he identified as a cloudlike smear. Only in 1924 did American astronomer Edwin Hubble prove that Andromeda was another galaxy, making it the first galaxy outside the Milky Way to be identified.

The Local Group is about 9.8 million light-years across. It contains two smaller groups of galaxies—the Milky Way with its satellites and the Andromeda Galaxy with its satellites. The third-largest galaxy in the group, Triangulum, may be a satellite of Andromeda. It is the third and last spiral in the group, but it does not have a central bar.

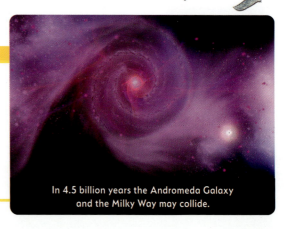

The constellation of Andromeda, its stars shown as gold dots, is pictured in Persian astronomer Abd al-Rahman al-Sufi's *Book of Fixed Stars*. The galaxy is just to the left of Princess Andromeda's belt.

The Andromeda Galaxy

Type: Barred spiral galaxy
Size: 220,000 light-years across
Number of stars: 1 trillion
Mass of supermassive black hole: The same as 110–230 million suns
Satellite galaxies: At least 19
Average distance from the sun: 2.5 million light-years

In 4.5 billion years the Andromeda Galaxy and the Milky Way may collide.

32

In this photograph of the Andromeda Galaxy, one of its satellites, a dwarf elliptical galaxy called M110, can be seen as a bright oval to the lower left.

33

EXOPLANETS

An exoplanet is a planet outside our solar system. The first exoplanet was not discovered until 1992, but today we know of more than 5,000 exoplanets orbiting more than 3,000 stars. Most of the exoplanets confirmed so far are in the Milky Way, due to the difficulty of spotting planets at the great distances of other galaxies.

Many types of exoplanets have been found. There are small, rocky, Earthlike planets, as well as super-Earths, which are planets with up to 10 times the mass of Earth. There are also ice giants, made of similar materials to Neptune and Uranus, and gas giants like Jupiter and Saturn. Gas giants that orbit so close to their stars that they are very hot are known as hot Jupiters. Some exoplanets, called rogue planets, do not orbit a star. They may have been thrown out of a solar system, or they may have formed on their own.

Astronomers study exoplanets for signs they could be habitable, or suitable for life. To be habitable, a planet needs to be the right distance from its star for liquid water. As far as we know, liquid water is needed by all forms of life. If a planet is too close to a star, water will boil away, and if it is too distant, water will freeze. Many possibly habitable exoplanets have been found, but they are too far away for astronomers to know yet if life has evolved there.

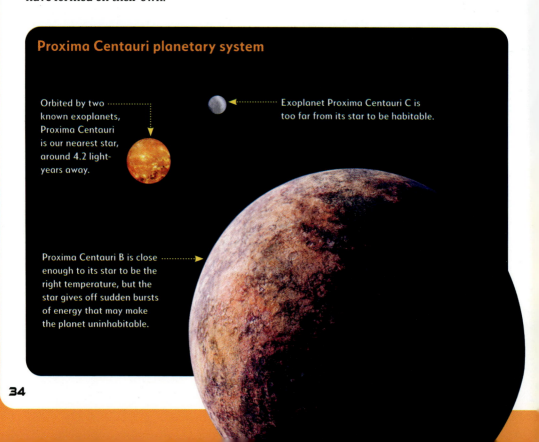

Proxima Centauri planetary system

Orbited by two known exoplanets, Proxima Centauri is our nearest star, around 4.2 light-years away.

Exoplanet Proxima Centauri C is too far from its star to be habitable.

Proxima Centauri B is close enough to its star to be the right temperature, but the star gives off sudden bursts of energy that may make the planet uninhabitable.

Exoplanet Luyten b

Luyten b is a super-Earth that orbits at a habitable distance from its star.

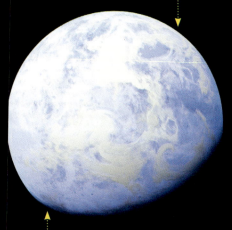

At just 12 light-years away, Luyten b is one of the closest possibly habitable exoplanets.

Exoplanet ROXs 42Bb

ROXs 42Bb is a hot Jupiter and one of the largest known exoplanets.

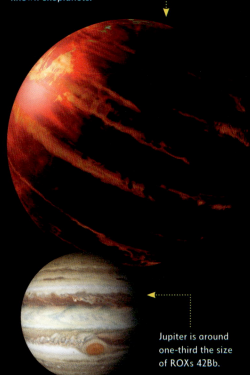

Jupiter is around one-third the size of ROXs 42Bb.

Trappist-1 Planetary System

About 40 light-years from Earth, Trappist-1 is a cool red dwarf star orbited by seven exoplanets.

Trappist-1b and Trappist-1c are too close to their star to be habitable.

Exactly the right distance from its star, Trappist-1e is an Earthlike planet that could be habitable.

Trappist-1g and Trappist-1h are so far from their star they may be covered by ice and uninhabitable.

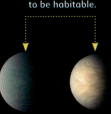   

Trappist-1d is just cool enough to be habitable but may have a poisonous atmosphere.

Trappist-1f may have a super-deep steamy ocean.

35

THE ANTENNAE GALAXIES

The Antennae Galaxies are a pair of interacting galaxies. This means that the galaxies are being affected by each other's gravity. The galaxies get their name from the long trails of stars, gas, and dust thrown out by the interaction. These trails look a little like an insect's curving antennae.

Interaction between two galaxies may be minor, such as when a satellite galaxy attracts the arm of the large galaxy it orbits. A more major interaction can result in what's known as galaxy cannibalism—when a large galaxy drags away all the stars from a satellite. In the case of the Antennae Galaxies, the two galaxies are colliding. Most galaxies collide with another at some point. Even our Milky Way will one day join with the Andromeda Galaxy.

Before the collision, the Antennae Galaxies, known as NGC 4038 and NGC 4039, were both spiral galaxies. About 600 million years ago, the two galaxies crashed into each other, causing the two trails of stars to be thrown out by conflicting pulls of gravity. This is how the antennae were formed.

At the moment, both galaxies are going through the starburst phase, which is when many stars form at once. The collision of dust and gas clouds is causing clumps that grow, get hotter, and turn into stars. In another 400 million years, the cores of the two galaxies will join. At that time, the galaxies will be merged as one giant elliptical galaxy.

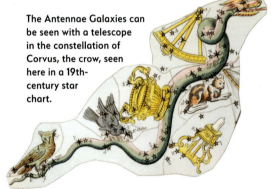

The Antennae Galaxies can be seen with a telescope in the constellation of Corvus, the crow, seen here in a 19th-century star chart.

The Antennae Galaxies

Type: Interacting galaxies
Size: 500,000 light-years across
Number of stars: 300 billion
Mass of supermassive black holes: Not known
Satellite galaxies: None known
Average distance from the sun: 45 million light-years

The galaxies' long antennae can be seen through a powerful amateur telescope.

Star-forming regions of the Antennae Galaxies shine blue among patches of hot hydrogen gas, shown in pink.

CENTAURUS A

When dust, gas, and stars are sucked into the supermassive black hole at the heart of the Centaurus A galaxy, powerful jets of energy shoot out. Much of this energy is in the form of X-rays and radio waves, which makes Centaurus A a radio galaxy. Radio galaxies are a type of active galaxy.

Although most galaxies have a supermassive black hole at their core, the black hole in an active galaxy is particularly busy. It drags in material from the galaxy's central region. The material spins around and around the black hole, getting extremely hot. This throws out beams of energy.

A radio galaxy is a type of active galaxy that emits energy we detect as radio waves. A quasar is an active galaxy that emits light, radio waves, and other energy. Quasars are the brightest objects in the universe, brighter than all the stars in the Milky Way, but almost all of them are too distant to be seen with amateur telescopes. A blazar is an active galaxy with an energy jet pointing straight at us.

The closest active galaxy to Earth, Centaurus A, is about 11 million light-years away. It is believed that early in the universe, most galaxies were active, but they have since quieted down. The reason why active galaxies are all so far away is that we are seeing these galaxies as they were when they were much younger. The more distant the object, the longer its light takes to reach us. We are seeing Centaurus A as it was 11 million years ago.

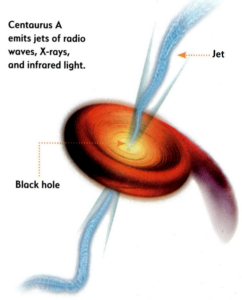

Centaurus A emits jets of radio waves, X-rays, and infrared light.

Jet

Black hole

Centaurus A
Type: Radio galaxy
Size: 60,000 light-years across
Number of stars: 300 billion
Mass of supermassive black hole: The same as 5 million suns
Satellite galaxies: At least 16
Average distance from the sun: 11 million light-years

This close-up shows the dark dust and glowing star clusters of a region of Centaurus A that is 8,500 light-years wide.

This image, created by an X-ray telescope and a visible light telescope, shows Centaurus A's energy jets in blue.

THE LANIAKEA SUPERCLUSTER

The Milky Way is a member of the Local Group of galaxies, which forms part of the Virgo Supercluster. This supercluster is just one portion of an even more immense cluster called the Laniakea Supercluster, which contains 100,000 galaxies. *Laniakea* means immense heaven in Hawaiian.

At the Laniakea Supercluster's heart is a region called the Great Attractor, which has a huge gravitational pull. In the illustration opposite, the Laniakea is shaded in gold, while known galaxies are shown as dots. The lines show the directions in which galaxies are being pulled toward the Great Attractor, where the brightest lines cross.

Despite the pull of the Great Attractor, the Laniakea Supercluster is expanding. The universe itself is expanding and, as it grows, so do superclusters. Like dots drawn on a balloon that is being blown up, the galaxy groups inside a supercluster get farther away from one another.

There may be about 10 million superclusters in the universe. Superclusters are not evenly spread through the universe. There are voids, or areas of nearly empty space, between them. Superclusters collect together in incredibly long threads called filaments. This gives the universe a structure a little like a sponge. The structure was caused by rippling differences in temperature as the universe expanded after the Big Bang.

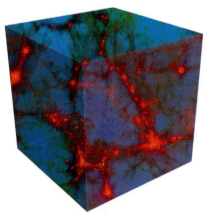

This illustration shows how galaxies (shown in red) are grouped into filaments in a cube of space billions of light-years across.

Laniakea

Type: Supercluster
Size: 520 million light-years across
Number of galaxies: 100,000
Mass: The same as 100 quadrillion (1 followed by 17 zeros) suns
Distance of the Great Attractor from the sun: 250 million light-years

The Great Attractor lies in this region of sky, in the Southern Triangle constellation.

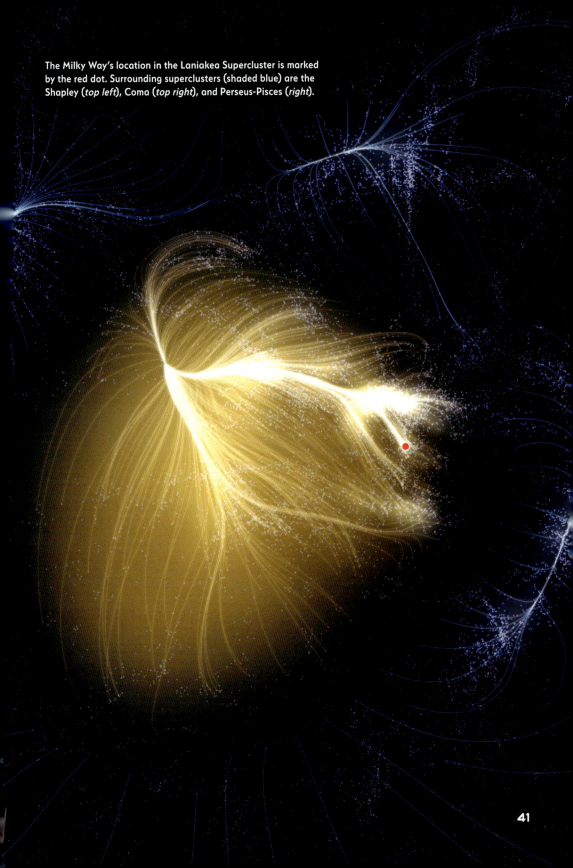

The Milky Way's location in the Laniakea Supercluster is marked by the red dot. Surrounding superclusters (shaded blue) are the Shapley (*top left*), Coma (*top right*), and Perseus-Pisces (*right*).

AN EXPANDING FUTURE

As our universe stretched and cooled following the Big Bang, the mass of objects it contained—stars, planets, gases, and dust—slowed the expansion due to the force of their gravity. Still, it did not stop expanding. As it grew, the mass of the objects contained within it decreased. At the same time, dark energy, an anti-gravity empty space that pushes matter away instead of attracting it, has remained constant.

The effect has been that the universe's expansion is again speeding up. If this expansion continues forever, galaxies will spread further apart from one another. All of the galaxies we can currently observe may slip far beyond our ability to detect. Our Milky Way Galaxy may be alone, the only star-spangled galaxy we will be able to see.

If this were to occur, it would be billions of years into the future. And this is only one theory of how the universe will continue to change and evolve. We are learning more new, exciting, mind-blowing things about our planet, our sun, our solar system, our galaxy, and our universe every day. And the tools we use for observing and exploring deep space are becoming ever more powerful and far-reaching.

We are lucky to be living in a time of such scientific advancement. With the help of powerful telescopes, space probes, and computers, we are beginning to have the ability to cast our gazes at the farthest edges of the visible universe. In so doing, we are catching awe-inspiring glimpses of how it all began and how it may end . . . if it ever does!

REVIEW AND REFLECT

Now that you've read about stars and galaxies, let's review what you've learned. Use the following questions to reflect on your newfound knowledge and integrate it with what you already knew.

Check for Understanding

1. What is a star? *(See p. 8)*

2. How does gravity affect stars? *(See p. 8)*

3. Describe one thing that's happening inside the sun. *(See p. 12)*

4. Name one example of solar activity. *(See p. 14)*

5. How and where does a new star form? *(See p. 16)*

6. What do scientists think will happen to the Pleiades, or the Seven Sisters, in the next 250 million years? *(See p. 18)*

7. How many stars can be in a star system? *(See pp. 20-21)*

8. What are three parts of a black hole? *(See p. 24)*

9. Describe the three shapes of galaxies. *(See pp. 28-29)*

10. Name two facts about the Milky Way. *(See pp. 30-32)*

11. Which galaxy was named after a princess from a Greek myth? *(See p. 32)*

12. Name two exoplanets and describe something we know about each. *(See pp. 34-35)*

13. What makes a planet habitable? *(See pp. 34-35)*

14. The Antennae Galaxies are interacting galaxies. What does that mean? *(See p. 36)*

15. Explain what an active galaxy is. Then, name three kinds of active galaxies. *(See p. 38)*

44

Making Connections

1. Choose three types of stars to compare and contrast. Name two characteristics of each.

2. How is a star system like a star cluster? How is it different?

3. In your own words, how would you describe a nebula?

4. Choose two galaxies mentioned in the book. What do they have in common? In what ways are they different?

5. Based on what you've learned about stars, what are some things that might happen to our sun in the future?

In Your Own Words

1. What can people on Earth learn from studying planets, galaxies, and stars? Why is that knowledge valuable or important?

2. How do astronomers choose names for objects or areas in space? Do you think these methods are good ways to name things? Why or why not?

3. How do you think the universe might evolve in the future?

4. Which details in this book were most interesting to you? What made them interesting?

5. What would you like to learn about stars and galaxies that we don't already know?

GLOSSARY

astronomer a scientist who studies the planets, stars, and other objects in space

atmosphere the gases surrounding a planet or moon, held by its gravity

atom the smallest unit of matter containing a central nucleus with particles called protons and neutrons, usually surrounded by one or more electrons

black hole an area of space with such strong gravity that no matter or light can escape from it

core the inner part of a planet or moon

electric charge a positive or negative quantity of electricity; electrons are negatively charged particles and protons are positively charged particles

electric current the flow of electrically charged particles

energy the power to do work that produces light, heat, or motion

exoplanet a planet outside our solar system

galaxy a group of millions or billions of stars, as well as gas and dust, that is held together by gravity

gas a substance that is not solid, liquid, or plasma; gas will expand to fill any container

gravity a force that pulls all objects and particles toward one another; the greater an object's mass, the greater the pull of its gravity

helium the second most common and second lightest element in the universe

hydrogen the most common and lightest element in the universe

infrared a type of energy given off by objects, which humans can feel as heat

light-year the distance that light travels in 1 year; 1 light-year is 5.88 trillion miles (9.46 trillion km)

magnetism a force caused by the movement of an electric charge, resulting in pulling and pushing forces between objects

mass a measure of the amount of matter in an object

matter a physical substance, in the form of a solid, liquid, gas, or plasma

moon a rounded object that orbits a planet

nebula a cloud of gas and dust

orbit the curved path of an object around a star, planet, or moon

oxygen the third most common element in the universe

planet an object orbiting a star that is massive enough for its gravity to pull it into a ball and to push or pull other objects out of its path

plasma an electrically charged gas made of free electrons and atoms that have lost electrons

solar system a sun and all the planets and other objects in orbit around it

star a glowing ball of plasma, held together by its own gravity

READ MORE

Fazekas, Andrew, James Trefil, Maya Wei-Haas, Rachel Brown, and Michael Greshko. *National Geographic Stargazer's Atlas: The Ultimate Guide to the Night Sky.* Washington, D.C.: National Geographic, 2022.

Green, Joel. *Black Holes (Tech Bytes: Exploring Space).* Chicago: Norwood House Press, 2023.

Miller, Ron. *The Big Backyard: The Solar System Beyond Pluto.* Minneapolis: Twenty-First Century Books, 2023.

Wiseman, Blaine. *Earth and the Stars (Space Systems: Stars and the Solar System).* New York: Smartbook Media/Lightbox, 2021.

LEARN MORE ONLINE

1. Go to **www.factsurfer.com** or scan the QR code below.
2. Enter **"Stars Galaxies"** into the search box.
3. Click on the cover of this book to see a list of websites.

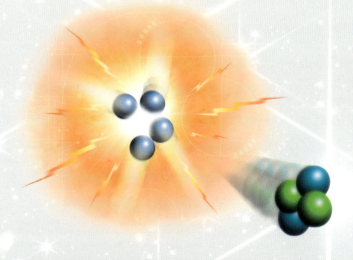

INDEX

Aldebaran 11,
Alpha Centauri 8, 21
al-Sufi, Abd al-Rahman 32
Andromeda Galaxy 32–33, 36
Antennae Galaxies 36–37
Betelgeuse 11
Big Bang 4, 6–7, 40, 42
black holes 24–26, 31–32, 38,
blazars 38
Cannon, Annie Jump 8
Centaurus A galaxy 38–39
Clown Face Nebula 22
dark energy 7, 42
dark matter 26
Eagle Nebula 16
Earth 4, 7, 12, 14, 16, 18, 26–28, 30–31, 34–35, 38
exoplanets 34–35
galaxies 4, 7, 20, 24–34, 36, 38, 40, 42
gas giants 34
Gemini 22
gravity 8, 10, 16, 18, 24, 26, 28–29, 32, 36, 42
Hoag's Object 29
Hubble Space Telescope 9, 21
ice giants 34
interacting galaxies 36
Jupiter 34–35
Laniakea Supercluster 26, 40–41
life 10, 12, 22, 24, 34
light 4, 6, 8–9, 12–13, 15–16, 18, 21–22, 24, 26–28, 30–32, 34–36, 38–40

Local Group 26, 32, 40
magnetism 14
Mercury 12
Milky Way Galaxy 22, 25, 30–31
moons 4
Neptune 34
Oort Cloud 21
Orion 10–11, 30
Pinwheel Galaxy 28
planetary nebulae 22
radio galaxy 38
Rubin, Vera 26
satellite galaxies 30, 32–33, 36
Saturn 34
Seven Sisters 18–19
Sirius 21
Solar System 26
stars 4, 7–12, 14, 16–26, 28, 30–32, 34–36, 38, 42
sun 7–8, 10, 12–15, 18, 22, 26–27, 30–31, 35
superclusters 26, 40–41
supernova 24
telescopes 36, 38–39, 42
universe 4, 8, 26
Uranus 34
Venus 12
Whirlpool Galaxy 27
white dwarf 10, 12, 20–23

48